Cooking for Two

Delicious Food Fast

> Author: **Cornelia Adam** | Photos: **Michael Brauner**

Contents

Theory

The Recipes

Appendix

Meals without Stress

So you want good, healthy food, but you want your cooking to be stress-free? Then these recipes are for you: Practical, fast dishes for every day with ingredients you can find in any supermarket, plus a few extravagant dishes for weekends. How about a romantic candlelight dinner on Saturday night and a cozy brunch on Sunday? Use this book for excellent ideas and inspiration for user-friendly cooking.

Well Planned is Half the Battle

1 | Rational Planning

Make a brief plan for the coming week's meals, preferably over the weekend when you have some free time. While you're at it, think about how often you will eat at home and how many nights you'll want to eat out—this will help you to only buy the ingredients you need, minimizing waste. Next, schedule time for shopping and cooking. Being well-organized will save you time, energy, and money.

2 | Sensible Shopping

Before your shopping excursion, make a list only of what you need. It's best to arrange it by products listed under the shops in which you buy them. You might want to make some of your purchases in the morning, during your lunch break, or late at night when the stores aren't as crowded, if that is of concern to you. Try to buy fruit, vegetables, meat, and bread fresh daily (or on days you're cooking) so they'll be at their best with regard to taste, appearance, and ingredients. In the case of canned goods, frozen foods, and dried staples, you need only buy them on a weekly or monthly basis in larger quantities. One final tip is to take a cooler along for stowing your frozen and refrigerated purchases, to keep them at their best during the trip home.

3 | Cooking Tips and Tricks

There are few things more enjoyable than sharing good food with someone you love. But even the most delicious recipes are of little use if you come home after a long day's work only to spend an eternity in the kitchen. Following are cooking hints that will save you time, effort, and wear-and-tear on your nerves, while leaving you more time for your partner—lest your dinner conversation consist mostly of yawns:

➤ Rice, pasta, and potatoes are classic side dishes. You may as well double the amount you cook each time since all of these can be saved for future meals (just don't freeze the potatoes). For example, boiled potatoes can be served up to two days later as fried potatoes or in a potato omelet. And, pasta or rice can be used in salads, soups, or vegetable dishes.

➤ For any dishes that can be frozen, make extra and freeze the remainder in serving-size containers or bags.

➤ Unless otherwise specified in this book's recipes, cover pots and pans with their lids while cooking. The food will cook faster and the cooking will require less power.

➤ Try to cut meat or vegetables into uniform-sized cubes; this ensures all parts of the dish will finish cooking at the same time.

➤ Even if you're on a tight budget, invest in kitchen tools that will make your job considerably easier. The essentials include an electric hand mixer (or stand mixer), a food processor, a blender, a hand blender, and a set of good knives for cutting meat and vegetables. For functional knives, sharpness is essential.

Quick Takes

Clear Soups

(Using canned broths or stocks)

➤ Sprinkle in any of the following as desired: rice, vermicelli, chopped vegetables, chicken or salmon strips, shrimp, and freshly chopped herbs. Boil gently until cooked to your taste.

➤ Clear beef broth tastes excellent with a shot of Sherry or Madeira.

Heartier Soups, Sauces, and Stews

(Using prepared products)

➤ Season creamy soups with white wine, vermouth, calvados, sherry, or lemon juice.

➤ Enhance Asian soups with coconut milk, rice wine, soy sauce, or saffron.

➤ Sprinkle soups with fresh herbs, peeled-and-cooked shrimp, or strips of smoked salmon.

➤ Stir in cream, crème fraîche, or heavy cream for a more decadent meal.

Vegetables

(Using frozen or canned)

➤ Create an Asian vegetable medley using coconut milk, ginger, and soy sauce as enhancements. Bacon crumbles or small cubes of salami can turn vegetables into more substantial dishes.

➤ Sprinkle vegetables with grated cheese, brown under the oven broiler, and serve.

➤ Vegetables can be mixed with ham, sausage, poultry, or fish as desired.

➤ Purée cooked vegetables with broth to make a soup and add cream as a finishing touch.

Mashed Potatoes

(Using the instant variety)

➤ Purée cooked broccoli, spinach, or beets and mix with the cooked mashed potatoes.

➤ For a faster, hearty version, stir in fried (or roasted) garlic, diced cooked bacon, or sautéed onions.

Rice

(Using leftover rice)

➤ Toss with butter and saffron (or curry powder). This idea for rice is especially good with fish or with Asian dishes. Even better: add a little freshly grated (or minced) ginger.

Lettuce

(Using prepackaged and ready-to-eat types)

To turn salad greens into a small meal or tasty appetizer, add: tuna, cubed ham, feta cheese, pitted kalamata olives, croutons, hard-boiled eggs, smoked salmon, or smoked trout. Finish off with a bottle of homemade vinaigrette.

Pantry Success Stories

Tomatoes, the canned variety, work great in soups and sauces.

➤ Pasta with Tomato-Caper Sauce

Finely chop 1 onion and 1 clove of garlic and sauté briefly in 1 tbs olive oil. Add 1 can (14 oz) peeled, diced tomatoes with their juice, and simmer uncovered over high heat for 10 minutes. Season with salt, pepper, and dried oregano; and stir in $1/4$ cup drained and rinsed capers. Cook 8 oz pasta in salted water until al dente; drain, mix with tomato-caper sauce, and sprinkle with grated Parmesan.

➤ Tomato Soup with Salami

Briefly sauté 1 finely chopped onion and 3 oz diced salami in 1 tbs olive oil. Add 1 large can (26 oz) peeled tomatoes (diced or whole) including liquid and mash with a fork or potato masher. Bring to a boil, then simmer for 10 minutes. Season to taste with salt, pepper, and dried thyme.

Pastry dough is available frozen, refrigerated, or as a mix.

➤ Pear Tart

Preheat oven to 425°F. Stack 2 thawed sheets (about 3 oz each) of puff pastry, one on top of the other, and roll out. Place on a baking sheet covered with parchment paper. Peel 3 pears, remove and discard cores, cut into thin wedges, and arrange on top of pastry. Combine 8 oz sour cream, 2 egg yolks, $1/3$ cup powdered sugar, and 1 pinch cinnamon. Distribute mixture on pears and bake tart for 20 minutes, until pastry is golden.

➤ Camembert in Puff Pastry

Thaw about 8 oz frozen puff pastry. Preheat oven to 425°F. Stack pastry sheets on top of one another, roll out, and cut into quarters. Cut a wedge of camembert cheese into quarters, place one piece on each piece of pastry, season with pepper, and wrap up. Place on a baking sheet covered with parchment paper. Combine 1 egg yolk and 2 tbs cream. Brush onto puff pastry and bake for 15 minutes.

Pasta can be purchased fresh from the refrigerated section. This reduces the cooking time by several minutes.

➤ Pasta Gratin

Cook 8 oz pasta in salted water until al dente. Chop 3 oz salami or ham, mix with pasta, and pour into a greased baking dish. Combine 7 tbs cream (or crème fraîche) and $3 1/2$ oz grated cheese, distribute over pasta, and bake (oven pre-heated to 375°F) for 15 minutes.

➤ Pasta Salad

Cook 8 oz of small pasta (e.g., farfalle, penne) in salted water until al dente; drain. Add $1/3$ lb cooked sausage (or cured salami) and $1/2$ lb of any chopped, cooked vegetable plus 1 minced green onion, 1 minced clove garlic, and pitted olives or herbs as desired. For the dressing, combine 3 tbs vinegar, $1/4$ cup olive oil, salt, and pepper; toss with other ingredients. Check salt to taste and chill before serving.

Canned tuna is sometimes packed in oil. If you prefer fewer calories, buy tuna packed in water.

➤ Tuna-Pesto Crostini

Drain 1 can tuna and purée in a blender with $1/4$ cup pesto (prepared product). Toast baguette slices and spread with the purée.

➤ Pasta with Tuna-Onion Sauce

Finely chop 1 large onion and sauté in 2 tbs butter until tender. Add 1 cup vegetable stock, $1/4$ cup crème fraîche, and 1 can drained tuna; purée everything with a hand blender. Simmer uncovered for 5 minutes. Season to taste with salt, pepper, and lemon juice. Cook 8 oz pasta in salted water until al dente, drain, and mix with sauce. Garnish with fresh herbs.

Peas are available frozen.

➤ Pea Salad

Cook $2/3$ cup long-grain rice in salted water for 15 minutes; drain. Blanch 1 cup frozen peas in salted water for 3 minutes. In a bowl, combine peas, rice, and 1 can tuna (drained and shredded). Make a dressing from 3 tbs mayonnaise, 3 tbs vinegar, 1 tbs oil, salt, and pepper. Add 2 chopped green onions and toss with salad. Serve chilled.

➤ Pasta Gratin with Peas

Preheat oven to 375°F. Blanch $1 1/3$ cups frozen peas in boiling salted water. Cook $1/3$ lb pasta in salted water. Combine 3 oz grated cheese and $1/3$ cup heavy cream. Season with salt, pepper, and nutmeg. Pour pasta and peas into a greased baking dish, pour cheese mixture over the top and bake on the middle rack for 15 minutes.

Cheese can be purchased at a cheese counter or packaged in the refrigerated section.

➤ Cheese Salad

Dice $1/2$ lb hard cheese. Mince 2 green onions or shallots (or 1 very small white or red onion). Peel 2 pears, dice, and sprinkle with lemon juice; combine with cheese and onion. Make a dressing from 2 tbs vinegar, 3 tbs oil, $1/2$ tsp prepared mustard, salt, and pepper; pour over other ingredients and stir. Chopped walnuts and/or herbs can also be added.

➤ Creamy Cheese Soup

Bring 2 cups stock or broth to a boil. Add 6 oz of a mixture of the following: cream cheese, goat cheese chèvre, Gorgonzola, Roquefort, or whole ricotta (do not use lowfat nor nonfat cheeses). Stir over low heat until all the cheese has melted. Season to taste with salt and pepper. Sprinkle with chopped herbs if desired.

Short and Sweet Desserts

Coconut-Laced Melon

1 melon (cantaloupe
or honeydew)
2 tbs slivered almonds
Juice of 1 lime
6 tbs coconut milk
2 tbs white rum (optional)
3 tbs sugar
2 sprigs mint

Peel melon, cut into
quarters, and dice. Toast
slivered almonds (dry
pan over medium heat,
stirring until golden).
Combine lime juice,
coconut milk, rum, and
sugar. Mix in diced
melon and slivered
almonds. Rinse mint,
pluck off leaves and
sprinkle on top.

Blueberry Sorbet

3 cups frozen blueberries
3 tbs powdered sugar

Thaw blueberries
slightly and purée in a
blender. Stir in powdered
sugar and spoon into
small dessert bowls. If
desired, garnish with
mint leaves or a dollop
of whipped cream.
Alternatively, a little
sparkling wine or
champagne can be
poured over the top.

White Wine Peaches

1¼ cups white wine
1 cinnamon stick
3 whole cloves
¼ cup sugar
2 ripe peaches
¼ cup crème fraîche

Bring white wine to a
boil with cinnamon stick,
cloves, and sugar. Mean-
while, boil some water
and submerge peaches
in it; rinse peaches
under cold water, peel,
halve, and remove pits.
Place peaches in wine
mixture and simmer for
5 minutes, then remove.
Simmer and reduce wine
mixture by half. Stir in
crème fraîche and serve
over peaches.

Raspberry Tiramisu

2½ cups frozen raspberries
8 oz mascarpone cheese
¼ cup sugar
8 ladyfingers
¼ cup raspberry brandy,
kirsch, or fruit juice
½ cup chopped pistachios

Cook raspberries over
medium heat for 5 minutes,
process in a food processor,
and strain. Combine strained
raspberries with mascar-
pone and sugar (add more
sugar to taste). Place 4
ladyfingers in a bowl and
drizzle with half the raspberry brandy. Top with half
the raspberry-mascarpone
mixture. Repeat layers
until all ingredients have
been used. Sprinkle top
with pistachios.

Creamy Rice with Plums

$1/2$ cup instant rice
$1/3$ cup sour cream (or crème fraîche)
3 tbs powdered sugar
2 tbs sugar
1 tsp vanilla
16 oz canned plums (or other canned fruit)
1 pinch cinnamon

Prepare rice according to package directions and let cool. Combine sour cream, powdered sugar, sugar, and vanilla; fold into rice. Heat plums with their juice until most of the liquid evaporates. Stir in cinnamon, let cool, and top creamy rice mixture with plums.

Amaretti and Berries

$3/4$ cup mixed berries (fresh or frozen)
2 tbs fruit brandy (optional; e.g., kirsch)
$3/4$ cup or about 5 amaretti cookies
2 cups sour cream or crème fraîche
3 tbs honey
2 tbs fresh lemon juice

Rinse berries and drain, then drizzle with fruit brandy. Chop amaretti cookies in a food processor. Stir cookies together with sour cream, honey, and lemon juice. To serve, top creamy mixture with berries.

Thick Cherry Crêpe

16 oz canned cherries
2 eggs
1 cup flour
3 tbs sugar
$1/2$ cup milk
2 tbs ground hazelnuts
2 tbs canola oil

Drain cherries. Separate eggs. Combine egg yolks, flour, sugar, milk, and hazelnuts. Beat egg whites until stiff and fold into batter. Fold in cherries. In a pan, heat oil, pour in batter, and cook over low heat for about 10 minutes, turning once. Cut into wedges for serving.

Sautéed Caramel Apples

2 large apples
1 tbs butter
1 pinch cinnamon
$1/2$ cup sugar
$2/3$ cup cream

Peel apples, cut into eighths, and remove cores. In a pan, melt butter and sauté apple wedges for 5 minutes. Dust with cinnamon and transfer to two plates. Melt sugar in the pan and let it turn golden. Pour in cream and simmer for 3 minutes. Pour over apples and serve while warm.

Brunch—The Morning Treat

Start by sleeping late and then treat yourselves to a cozy brunch—a generous gourmet-style breakfast. The great part about brunch is that it combines both breakfast and lunch elements. Instead of the same old breakfast doldrums, it consists of small, hearty dishes that are quickly prepared or made in advance. Give yourself this wonderful treat, and not only on special occasions! Some of the combinations might even work for breakfast in bed.

Quick Recipes

Melon with Mango Cream

SERVES 2:

➤ 1 small honeydew melon | 1 ripe mango | 1 tbs honey | 1 tsp fresh lemon juice | 8 oz sour cream or crème fraîche (lowfat OK) | 2 tsp chopped pistachios

1 | Cut melon into quarters, remove seeds, peel and slice into narrow wedges. Arrange in an overlapping pattern.

2 | Peel mango. Cut fruit away from pit and purée in a blender with honey and lemon juice.

3 | Stir mango mixture together with sour cream or crème fraîche. Place a dollop next to the honeydew wedges; sprinkle with pistachios.

Artichoke-Feta Spread

SERVES 2:

➤ 1 can artichoke hearts (about 10 oz after draining) | 1 clove garlic | ³/₄ cup fresh parsley sprigs | 5 oz feta cheese | 1 tbs fresh lemon juice | 1 pinch cumin | Salt and pepper

1 | Squeeze out artichoke hearts thoroughly; drain. Peel garlic. Rinse parsley and discard tough stems.

2 | Purée artichokes, garlic, parsley, and feta in a blender. Season with lemon juice, salt, pepper, and cumin. Serve with celery sticks, crackers, and/or toasted baguette slices.

Healthy | Fast

Oatmeal with Berries and Almonds

SERVES 2:

- ➤ **2 tbs slivered almonds**
  1½ cups raspberries
  1½ cups blueberries
  1 tsp fresh lemon juice
  1½ cups cooked oatmeal
  8 oz yogurt
  2 tbs honey

🕐 Prep time: 10 minutes
➤ Calories per serving: About 440

1 | Toast slivered almonds in a nonstick pan without oil until golden brown. Stir constantly to avoid burning. Set aside.

2 | Rinse berries briefly and drain. Drizzle with fresh lemon juice. In a bowl, combine cooked oatmeal, yogurt, and honey. Fold in berries. Transfer mixture to two bowls and sprinkle with slivered almonds.

➤ Variation: Depending on the season, you can use other combinations of fruit. Instead of almonds, try pistachios, sliced hazelnuts, or sesame seeds.

Simple | Classy

Banana-Coconut Breakfast Wedges

SERVES 2:

- ➤ **1 large ripe banana**
  1 tsp fresh lemon juice
  8 oz lowfat sour cream
  2 eggs
  1 cup flour
  1 pinch salt
  2 tbs sugar
  2 tbs grated coconut
  3 tbs butter
  3 tbs powdered sugar

🕐 Prep time: 30 minutes
➤ Calories per serving: About 730

1 | Peel banana, cut into somewhat thick slices, and drizzle with lemon juice.

2 | Combine sour cream, eggs, flour, salt, sugar, and grated coconut. Using a hand mixer, blend into a smooth mixture and then stir in bananas.

3 | Melt half the butter in a small-to-medium nonstick pan, heat, and add sour cream mixture. Fry over medium heat for about 10 minutes until golden-brown on the first side.

4 | Slide onto a plate, melt remaining butter in pan, flip over pancake and fry for another 10 minutes on the other side. Slide onto a plate, sprinkle with powdered sugar and cut into pie-like wedges.

TIP

This dish is delicious with a raspberry sauce (puree fresh or frozen raspberries with sugar and strain out seeds). It also tastes great cold, makes a fantastic dessert, and is ideal for picnics.

Easy

Arugula Scramble with Smoked Salmon

SERVES 2:

- ➤ 1 cup arugula leaves
- 3–4 oz sliced smoked salmon
- 4 eggs
- 2 tbs crème fraîche
- 1 pinch cayenne pepper
- 1 tsp fresh lemon juice
- 1 tbs butter
- Salt and pepper

⏱ Prep time: 30 minutes

➤ Calories per serving: About 425

1 | Rinse arugula, remove any tough stems, and chop. Cut smoked salmon into narrow strips.

2 | Break eggs into a bowl and whisk. Stir in crème fraîche and arugula. Season with salt, pepper, cayenne, and fresh lemon juice.

3 | In a nonstick pan, heat butter and pour in eggs. Let solidify slowly over low heat, stirring occasionally.

Distribute smoked salmon strips on top when almost done, to warm them through. Serve.

TIP

Serve on buttered toast. If you want, sprinkle with a little watercress or chopped chives. Not only does it look nice, but it tastes great. In lieu of salmon, try cooked shrimp, ham, tuna, or make a vegetarian version with chopped sun-dried tomatoes.

Hearty | Simple

Ham-n-Egg Cups

SERVES 2:

- ➤ 3–4 oz cooked sliced ham (thick slice)
- 8 fresh chive spears
- 4 eggs
- 1 pinch freshly grated nutmeg
- 2 tsp butter
- Salt and pepper

⏱ Prep time: 20 minutes

➤ Calories per serving: About 260

1 | Dice ham finely. Rinse chives, shake dry, and chop into fine rings.

2 | In a bowl, whisk eggs and season with salt, pepper, and nutmeg. Stir in chives and ham.

3 | Grease two individual baking cups or ramekins with butter and pour in egg mixture.

4 | Seal cups with aluminum foil and place in a wide pot. Pour hot water into the pot to just below the rims of the cups. Bring water to a boil and simmer gently for 10 minutes until the egg has set, testing doneness with your finger.

Italian | Hearty

Fennel-Mortadella Salad

SERVES 2:

- 2 fennel bulbs
  1 small onion or shallot
  $1/3$ cup olive oil
  3 tbs balsamic vinegar
  3 oz thinly sliced mortadella (deli counter)
  Salt and pepper

⏱ Prep time: 15 minutes
- Calories per serving: About 395

1 | Clean fennel. Remove greens and set aside. Rinse fennel bulb and peel onion. Using a kitchen slicer (mandoline) or very sharp knife, cut fennel and onion into very thin strips. Finely chop fennel greens.

2 | In a bowl, thoroughly mix olive oil, balsamic vinegar, salt, and pepper. Stir in fennel and onion strips and marinate briefly.

3 | Cut mortadella into thin strips, combine with fennel-onion mixture, and season to taste.

➤ Variation: Instead of mortadella, use cooked shrimp or tuna packed in olive oil.

Can Prepare in Advance

Artichokes with Cherry Tomatoes and Shrimp

SERVES 2:

- 1 can artichoke hearts (about 10 oz after draining)
  2 green onions
  $1/3$ lb cooked, peeled shrimp
  $1/2$ lb cherry tomatoes
  3 tbs olive oil
  2 tbs fresh lemon juice
  1 tbs pesto (prepared product)
  Lettuce leaves for garnish (optional)
  Salt and pepper

⏱ Prep time: 10 minutes
- Calories per serving: About 375

1 | Cut artichoke hearts into quarters and place in a bowl. Rinse green onions and slice into fine rings. Add green onions and shrimp to artichoke hearts. Rinse cherry tomatoes, cut in half, and fold into other ingredients.

2 | Stir together olive oil, fresh lemon juice, and pesto; season with salt and pepper and add to other ingredients. Mix well and add more salt to taste. If desired, arrange mixture on top of a few lettuce leaves.

TIP

If you're in a hurry, use marinated artichokes from a jar that are already quartered.

Low-Fat | Fast

Zucchini with Tuna

SERVES 2:

➤ ½ lb zucchini

1 shallot

1 clove garlic

½ cup fresh parsley sprigs

¼ cup olive oil

⅓ cup fresh lemon juice

1 can water-packed tuna (about 5 oz drained)

Salt and pepper

⏱ Prep time: 25 minutes

➤ Calories per serving: About 285

1 | Rinse zucchini and cut lengthwise into slices about ¼ inch thick, using a mandoline, very sharp knife, or vegetable peeler. Bring salted water to a boil and blanch zucchini slices for 30 seconds. Drain on paper towels.

2 | Peel shallot and garlic. Rinse parsley and discard any tough stems. Set aside several leaves and mince the rest finely along with shallot and garlic.

3 | Using a hand blender, blend together olive oil, fresh lemon juice, salt, and pepper. Mix shallot, garlic, and parsley into the dressing.

4 | Arrange zucchini slices casually on a platter. Drain tuna, shred as finely as possible with two forks and distribute over the zucchini slices. Pour dressing evenly over the top and garnish with remaining parsley.

Can Prepare in Advance | Classy

Smoked Fish in a Chive Cream

SERVES 2:

➤ 1 small onion

1 apple

2 tbs fresh lemon juice

⅓ cup sour cream

1 bunch chives

6 cleaned Matjes herring fillets (or equivalent of any smoked or preserved fish)

Salt and pepper

⏱ Prep time: 25 minutes

➤ Calories per serving: About 755

1 | Peel onion and chop coarsely. Peel apple, cut into quarters, remove core, and sprinkle with lemon juice to keep it from discoloring. In a blender, purée apple pieces, onion, and sour cream.

2 | Rinse chives and chop into fine rings. Transfer puréed sauce to a bowl and season with salt and pepper. Stir in chopped chives.

3 | Cut Matjes herring fillets (or other preserved fish) into narrow strips, place in a bowl and pour sauce over the top. Marinate in refrigerator until serving.

Lunch: Soups, Salads, and Snacks

Lunch is usually not the time for eating excessively or extravagantly. The best solution is light, tasty dishes that are small, simple, and quick to prepare—the perfect occasion for a cup of soup, a crispy salad, or a sandwich. If you're hungrier than that, combine all three! This chapter also includes snacks for taking on the run.

Quick Recipes

Vegetable Sticks with Garbanzo Bean Dip

SERVES 2:

➤ $^1\!/_2$ lb carrots | 1 cucumber | $^1\!/_2$ lb celery | 1 red bell pepper | 1 can garbanzo beans (about 14 oz) | $^3\!/_4$ cup fresh basil sprigs | 2 cloves garlic | $^1\!/_3$ cup olive oil | Cayenne pepper | 1 tsp fresh lemon juice | Salt and pepper

1 | Rinse carrots, cucumber, celery, and bell pepper; clean and cut into pieces about 2 inches long. Place vegetable sticks into a glass.

2 | Drain garbanzo beans. Rinse basil and discard any tough stems. Peel garlic. Purée these ingredients together with olive oil and season generously with salt, pepper, cayenne, and lemon juice. Serve with vegetable sticks.

Roast Beef Salad

SERVES 2:

➤ 1 bunch arugula | $^1\!/_2$ lb roast beef (medium) | 2 tbs fresh lemon juice | $^1\!/_4$ cup olive oil | Salt and pepper | 2 oz Parmesan

1 | Rinse arugula, remove any tough stems, and arrange casually on two plates along with roast beef.

2 | Combine lemon juice, olive oil, salt, and pepper in a bowl. Using a hand blender (or whisk), blend to form a creamy marinade. Drizzle over roast beef and arugula. Shave Parmesan over the top (try using a vegetable peeler).

Fiery Hot
Tacos with Steak Strips

SERVES 2:

➤ 1 small cucumber

1 beefsteak tomato (about ½ lb)

1 small onion

2 taco shells (prepared product)

1 beef tenderloin steak (about ½ lb)

2 tbs olive oil

1 pinch cumin

1 pinch chili powder

2-3 oz feta cheese

Salt and pepper

🕐 Prep time: 30 minutes

➤ Calories per serving: About 380

1 | Preheat oven to 375°F. Rinse cucumber and dice. Rinse tomato and cut into eighths. Peel onion and slice into fine rings.

2 | Heat taco shells according to package directions. Cut meat into narrow strips. In a wide pan, heat olive oil and sauté meat strips (about 5 minutes). Season with salt, pepper, cumin, and chili powder. Crumble feta.

3 | Fill taco shells with tomato wedges and diced cucumber and season with salt and pepper. Add cooked meat strips and sprinkle with feta.

Fast | Can Prepare in Advance
Salami Frittata with Peas

SERVES 2:

➤ 1 cup frozen peas

2 oz sliced salami

2 green onions

3 tbs olive oil

4 eggs

Salt and pepper

🕐 Prep time: 35 minutes

➤ Calories per serving: About 445

1 | Thaw and rinse peas. Finely dice salami. Rinse green onions, trim away root ends and slice thinly into rings. In a pan, heat half the olive oil and sauté green onions and salami for 5 minutes.

2 | Whisk eggs in a bowl. Season generously with salt and pepper and add the peas; stir. Pour over the salami and green onions in the pan; cook over medium heat and let solidify for no more than 10 minutes.

3 | Slide frittata onto a plate. Heat remaining olive oil in the pan, then flip over omelet, slide into the pan and cook for another 5 minutes or until cooked through.

Photo top: Tacos with Steak Strips   *Photo bottom:* **Salami Frittata with Peas** ➤

Asian | Low-Fat

Rice Paper Rolls with Vegetables and Wasabi Dip

SERVES 2:

- ➤ 2 oz cellophane (mung bean thread) noodles
  1 tbs toasted sesame oil
  ½ lb asparagus
  1 carrot
  1 cup arugula leaves
  4 rice paper wrappers (6–8 inch diameter round or 6x6 square)
  7 oz tofu
  3 tbs soy sauce
  3 tbs fresh lemon juice
  2 tsp wasabi (from a tube)
  Salt

🕐 Prep time: 30 minutes

➤ Calories per serving: About 280

1 | Pour boiling water over cellophane noodles and let stand for 5 minutes. Drain in a colander and let cool. Then cut into smaller pieces with kitchen scissors. Toss with sesame oil.

2 | Rinse asparagus and trim ends; peel lower third. Bring salted water to a boil and cook asparagus for 5 minutes or until crisp but tender. Pour into a colander, rinse under very cold water, and drain. Peel carrot and grate coarsely.

3 | Rinse arugula and cut off stems. Soften rice paper wrappers in lukewarm water one at a time for 1 minute each. Spread out on a cloth and pat slightly dry. Top with arugula first, then cellophane noodles, grated carrot, and asparagus.

4 | Roll rice paper wrappers tightly and cut each roll in half. For the dip, purée tofu, soy sauce, fresh lemon juice, and wasabi with a hand blender. Serve dip with rolls.

TIP Rolls will keep in the refrigerator for 2 days.

1 Spread

Spread wet rice paper wrappers on a clean cloth.

2 Fill

Top with vegetables and lay asparagus in the center.

3 Roll

Roll up rice paper wrappers tightly.

4 Cut

Cut in half diagonally with a sharp knife.

25

Can Prepare in Advance

Baguette with Pork Tenderloin and Tahini Dip

SERVES 2:

➤ ½ lb pork tenderloin
1 tsp fresh oregano
1 tbs fresh lemon juice
¼ cup olive oil
1 clove garlic
1 cup fresh basil sprigs
⅔ cup tahini (ground sesame paste; specialty market)
Juice of ½ lemon
2 small tomatoes
2 personal-size baguettes
Salt and pepper

🕐 Prep time: 25 minutes
➤ Calories per serving: About 930

1 | Cut pork into slices about ⅓ inch thick and press somewhat flat with the heel of your hand. Rinse oregano, pat dry, and pluck off leaves.

2 | Combine fresh lemon juice, 3 tbs of olive oil, and oregano leaves. Pour this marinade over the pork and mix well. Cover and marinate, refrigerated, for about 10 minutes.

3 | For the dip, peel garlic. Rinse basil and discard any tough stems. Purée these two ingredients (save a couple basil sprigs for garnish) with tahini, lemon juice, and the remaining olive oil. Season with salt and pepper.

4 | Pat meat slices dry and fry in a pan for a total of 10 minutes, turning once. Rinse tomatoes and slice. Cut open mini-baguettes and spread with tahini dip. Top with pork medallions and tomato slices in an overlapping pattern.

Easy

Ciabatta with Roquefort and Pear

SERVES 2:

➤ ¼ lb Roquefort
4 tbs butter (room temperature)
1 pinch freshly grated nutmeg
1 large pear
1 tsp fresh lemon juice
2 small ciabatta rolls
1 pinch cinnamon
Salt and pepper

🕐 Prep time: 10 minutes
➤ Calories per serving: About 550

1 | Place Roquefort and butter on a plate and mash finely with a fork until mixed. Season with salt, pepper, and nutmeg.

2 | Peel pear, cut lengthwise into quarters and remove core. Cut pear quarters lengthwise into thin slices and drizzle with fresh lemon juice.

3 | Cut ciabatta in half (toast if desired) and spread with Roquefort mixture. Decoratively arrange pear slices on top and sprinkle with a little cinnamon.

Hearty | Crispy

Green Leaf Lettuce with Bacon Mushrooms

SERVES 2:

➤ 3 strips smoked bacon
   1 shallot
   2 cloves garlic
   ½ lb mushrooms
   1 small head green leaf lettuce
   3 tbs sherry vinegar
   ¼ cup olive oil
   Salt and pepper

🕐 Prep time: 25 minutes

➤ Calories per serving: About 375

1 | Cut bacon into small cubes. Peel shallot and garlic; mince both. Rinse mushrooms and cut in half.

2 | In a small pan, fry the bacon until fat is rendered.

3 | Add mushrooms, shallot, and garlic to the pan and sauté for 5 minutes. Season with salt and pepper. Let cool.

4 | In the meantime, rinse lettuce, remove core, and drain leaves. Tear into bite-size pieces. In a bowl, beat sherry vinegar, olive oil, salt, and pepper to make a creamy dressing.

5 | Add bacon mushrooms to lettuce pieces and toss.

Light | Simple

Egg Salad with Herb Dressing

SERVES 2:

➤ 4 eggs
   A few sprigs each of parsley, chives, and basil
   1 sprig each of chervil and sorrel
   1 shallot
   1 clove garlic
   ½ lb cherry tomatoes
   2 tbs fresh lemon juice
   3 tbs olive oil
   Salt and pepper

🕐 Prep time: 25 minutes

➤ Calories per serving: About 325

1 | Hard-boil eggs for 10 minutes, rinse under ice-cold water, and let cool.

2 | Rinse herbs, discard any tough stems, and mince finely. Peel shallot and garlic; chop both finely. Rinse cherry tomatoes and cut in half.

3 | In a bowl, combine fresh lemon juice, olive oil, salt, and pepper; mix in the chopped herbs. Peel eggs, slice, and arrange in an overlapping pattern on two plates.

4 | Decoratively arrange cherry tomatoes on the eggs and drizzle evenly with herb dressing.

Classy | Exotic

Fish Salad with Bean Sprouts

SERVES 2:

➤ Juice of 1 lime
  $1/4$ cup oil
  1 tbs soy sauce
  1 clove garlic
  1 tiny piece fresh ginger ($1/2$-inch section)
  1 fresh red Fresno chile
  $1/2$ cup fresh cilantro sprigs
  1 red bell pepper
  $1^1/2$ cups fresh bean sprouts
  $1/2$ lb cod fillet
  Salt and pepper

🕐 Prep time: 30 minutes
➤ Calories per serving: About 340

1 | In a large bowl, combine lime juice, 2 tbs of the oil, and soy sauce. Peel garlic and ginger. Rinse chile and remove seeds. Mince garlic, ginger, and chile; add to bowl.

2 | Rinse cilantro and discard any tough stems. Rinse bell pepper, remove core and seeds, and cut into very fine, short strips. Place bean sprouts in a colander, pour boiling water over the top and drain. Add sprouts, cilantro leaves, and bell pepper strips to the bowl and toss with marinade.

3 | Cut cod into $3/4$-inch cubes. In a pan, heat remaining oil and sauté fish cubes for about 3 minutes. Season with salt and pepper, remove, and let cool slightly. Transfer salad to two plates, top with fish, and serve.

Mediterranean | Tangy

Pasta Salad with Gorgonzola

SERVES 2:

➤ $1/3$ lb small penne pasta
  1 small onion or shallot
  1 clove garlic
  $3/4$ cup arugula leaves
  $1/2$ cup basil leaves
  3 tbs white wine vinegar
  $1/4$ cup olive oil
  1 tsp prepared mustard
  $1/4$ lb Gorgonzola
  $1/2$ cup small black pitted olives (e.g., Niçoise or kalamata)
  Salt and pepper

🕐 Prep time: 25 minutes
➤ Calories per serving: About 685

1 | Bring salted water to a boil and cook pasta for no more than 10 minutes, until al dente. Pour into a colander, rinse under cold water, and drain.

2 | Peel onion and garlic and chop finely. Transfer to a bowl along with cooked pasta. Rinse arugula and basil, pluck off leaves, chop coarsely, and add to bowl.

3 | Whisk or beat together white wine vinegar, olive oil, mustard, salt, and pepper to make a creamy vinaigrette. Pour over other ingredients and toss.

4 | Dice Gorgonzola and stir into salad along with olives.

Fast | Can Prepare
in Advance

Middle-Eastern Carrot Soup with Couscous

SERVES 2:

➤ 1 shallot

1 tiny piece fresh ginger ($\frac{1}{2}$-inch section)

1 lb carrots

1 tbs butter

$2\frac{1}{4}$ cups vegetable stock

$\frac{3}{4}$ cup couscous

$\frac{1}{2}$ cup fresh cilantro sprigs

1 tbs fresh lemon juice

1 pinch cumin

Salt and pepper

🕐 Prep time: 30 minutes
➤ Calories per serving: About 300

1 | Peel shallot and ginger and chop both finely. Peel carrots and slice thinly. In a pot, heat butter and sauté these three ingredients for 5 minutes.

2 | Pour in vegetable stock, cover, and simmer for about 20 minutes until carrot slices are tender. Purée with a hand blender. Sprinkle couscous into purée; cover pan on very low heat until couscous becomes tender.

3 | In the meantime, rinse cilantro, pluck off leaves and chop finely. Season soup to taste with fresh lemon juice, salt, pepper, and cumin. Garnish with cilantro.

TIP In the summer, this soup can also be served chilled, topped with a dollop of sour cream or crème fraîche.

Exotic | Classy

Lentil Soup with Shrimp

SERVES 2:

➤ 3 cups vegetable stock

Several threads saffron

1 clove garlic

1 cup yellow lentils

1 carrot

2 tbs crème fraîche

$\frac{1}{4}$ lb cooked, peeled shrimp

1 tsp black sesame seeds

Salt and pepper

🕐 Prep time: 30 minutes
➤ Calories per serving: About 515

1 | In a pot, slowly bring vegetable stock to a boil with saffron (first crumble saffron between your fingers). Peel garlic and add with lentils to pot. Cover and simmer for 20 minutes. Meanwhile, peel and coarsely grate carrot.

2 | When lentils are cooked through, purée the lentil-stock mixture with a hand blender. Stir in crème fraîche and season with salt and pepper. Briefly heat shrimp and carrots in the soup.

3 | Pour soup into two bowls and garnish with black sesame seeds.

➤ Variation: Instead of saffron, you can use curry powder and replace the shrimp with freshly chopped herbs.

Hearty | Satisfying

Meat and Vegetable Stew

SERVES 2:

➤ ½ lb pork tenderloin
   3 slices smoked bacon
   1 small onion or shallot
   ½ lb carrots
   ½ lb small zucchini
   2 tbs oil
   1 cup frozen peas
   3 cups beef broth or stock
   1 bunch chives
   Salt and pepper

🕑 Prep time: 40 minutes
➤ Calories per serving:
   About 530

1 | Cut meat into cubes and bacon into short strips. Peel and chop onion. Peel and slice carrots. Rinse zucchini, trim ends, and dice.

2 | In a pot, heat oil and brown meat. Season with salt and pepper. Add onion, carrots, zucchini, and peas.

3 | Pour in meat stock, bring to a gentle boil, reduce heat to low, and simmer for 15 minutes. Meanwhile, rinse chives and chop finely.

4 | Season stew with salt and pepper and stir in chives.

Classy

Vegetable Soup with Avocado

SERVES 2:

➤ 1 small onion or shallot
   1 clove garlic
   2 tbs olive oil
   2 beefsteak tomatoes (about 1 lb)
   1 red bell pepper
   1⅔ cups vegetable stock
   1 ripe avocado
   1 tbs fresh lemon juice
   ½ cup fresh mint sprigs
   1 pinch cayenne pepper
   Salt and pepper

🕑 Prep time: 25 minutes
➤ Calories per serving:
   About 475

1 | Peel onion and garlic and chop finely. In a pot, heat olive oil and sauté onion and garlic over low heat.

2 | Pour boiling water over tomatoes, let sit for a minute, peel, and remove seeds. Remove seeds from bell pepper, rinse, and chop coarsely. Add tomatoes and pepper to pot and sauté briefly. Pour in vegetable stock and simmer for 10 minutes.

3 | Peel avocado, cut in half, and remove pit. Finely dice one half, drizzle with lemon juice and refrigerate. Chop remaining half coarsely, add to soup. Purée soup with a hand blender.

4 | Rinse mint, pluck off leaves, and finely chop all but a few for garnish. Season soup with salt, pepper, and cayenne. Stir in chopped mint. Sprinkle soup with diced avocado and garnish with mint leaves.

Simple and Delicious Dinners

Evenings are usually taken up by a trip to the gym, a movie, or gatherings with friends, leaving you little time for cooking. It's great to know how to prepare something quickly at home and eat in a relaxed manner. For dishes in this chapter, you'll find the necessary ingredients in any supermarket, and preparation is fast. If you're ever in the mood for something fancier (or want to entertain), add soup or salad as an appetizer and finish up with a dessert.

Quick Recipes

Gnocchi with Beet Sauce

SERVES 2:

➤ ½ lb beets (precooked or canned, but not pickled) | 1 shallot | 2 cloves garlic | 1 tbs olive oil | 1⅓ cups vegetable stock | 2 tbs crème fraîche | 1 lb gnocchi (prepared product) | 8 fresh chive spears | Salt and pepper

1 | Dice beets. Peel and chop shallot and garlic and sauté in olive oil. Add beets. Then add vegetable stock and crème fraîche. Simmer for 10 minutes. Cook gnocchi according to package directions. Rinse chives and chop finely.

2 | Purée vegetable stock mixture with a hand blender, season with salt and pepper, and stir in chives. Drain gnocchi and serve atop the sauce.

Salmon with Endive

SERVES 2:

➤ 1 onion | 1 lb endive | ¾ lb salmon fillet | 3 tbs oil | 1 cup vegetable stock | ⅓ cup crème fraîche | Juice of 1 orange | 1 tsp curry | Salt and pepper

1 | Peel onion and chop finely. Rinse endive, trim away core, and quarter remaining lengthwise. Rinse salmon under cold water, pat dry, and cut into cubes.

2 | Briefly sauté onion and endive in 2 tbs of the olive oil. Add vegetable stock, crème fraîche, and fresh orange juice; sauté on low for about 10 minutes. Season with salt, pepper, and curry.

3 | In a separate pan, sauté diced salmon in remaining olive oil for about 3 minutes, season to taste with salt and pepper, and serve alongside endive mixture.

Hearty | Fast

Chicken Breast in Gorgonzola Sauce

SERVES 2:

➤ 1 shallot
   4 tbs butter
   1 cup vegetable stock
   $\frac{1}{2}$ cup cream
   $\frac{1}{4}$ lb Gorgonzola
   1 tsp fresh lemon juice
   2 chicken breast fillets (about $\frac{1}{3}$ lb each)
   8 fresh chive spears
   $\frac{3}{4}$ lb sugar snap peas (or snow peas)
   Salt and pepper

⏱ Prep time: 25 minutes
➤ Calories per serving: About 720

1 | Peel shallot and chop finely. In a pot, heat 1 tbs of the butter and briefly sauté shallot. Pour in vegetable stock and cream and bring to a boil. Reduce heat to low.

2 | Dice Gorgonzola and add. Simmer for about 10 minutes, stirring occasionally. Season to taste with salt, pepper, and fresh lemon juice.
3 | In a pan, heat 2 tbs of the remaining butter and brown the chicken breast fillets on both sides. Keep cooking on medium until cooked through, opaque with no pink remaining, and juices run clear. Season with salt and pepper and let stand for a few minutes.

4 | Meanwhile, chop chives into fine rings. Clean sugar peas and blanch in salted water for 3 minutes. Toss with remaining butter. Season with salt and pepper and stir in chives.

5 | Slice chicken breasts and arrange on top of peas. Pour sauce over the top. Garnish with more chives if desired.

Exotic | Classy

Turkey in Mango Sauce

SERVES 2:

➤ 1 shallot
   1 ripe mango
   $\frac{3}{4}$ lb turkey breast
   2 tbs clarified butter (specialty store; or make your own by heating the butter and skimming and discarding the white solids)
   $\frac{1}{3}$ cup crème fraîche
   1 cup chicken stock
   1 pinch cayenne pepper
   1 pinch ground coriander
   1 tsp fresh lemon juice
   Salt and pepper

⏱ Prep time: 35 minutes
➤ Calories per serving: About 485

1 | Peel shallot and cut into quarters. Peel mango and cut fruit away from pit. Dice one third and set aside. Cut remaining mango and purée along with shallot wedges.

2 | Cut turkey breast into strips. In a pan, heat clarified butter and brown turkey strips. Season with salt and pepper, remove, and keep warm.

3 | Add mango purée, crème fraîche, and chicken stock to pan and simmer uncovered for about 5 minutes.

4 | Season sauce with salt, pepper, cayenne pepper, coriander, and fresh lemon juice. Add turkey to sauce and simmer for 5 minutes (make sure it's cooked through before serving). Season to taste and sprinkle with diced mango.

Impressive | Low-Cal
Lamb Fillet with Spinach

SERVES 2:

➤ ¾ lb lamb fillet
1 clove garlic
1 fresh red Fresno chile
1 shallot
½ lb spinach leaves
3 tbs olive oil
1 small cinnamon stick
¼ cup soy sauce
1¼ cups vegetable stock
1 tbs curry powder
Salt and pepper

🕐 Prep time: 30 minutes
➤ Calories per serving:
About 445

1 | Cut lamb fillet into ¾-inch cubes. Peel garlic and slice. Remove seeds from chile pepper, rinse, and chop finely. Peel shallot and chop finely. Rinse spinach well, remove any tough stems, and drain.

2 | In a wide pan or wok, heat half the olive oil. Sauté lamb cubes, garlic, chile pepper, and cinnamon stick for 5 minutes, then remove and set aside.

3 | Add remaining olive oil to the pan and sauté shallot and spinach for 5 minutes. Stir together soy sauce, vegetable stock, and curry powder; add to pan and bring to a boil. Return lamb mixture to the pan and simmer for 5 minutes or until cooked through.

Fast | Classy
Pork Tenderloin with Plums

SERVES 2:

➤ 3 tbs oil
¾ lb pork tenderloin
½ tsp dried thyme
½ lb plums
1 onion
1 cup beef stock or broth
3 tbs crème fraîche
1 pinch cinnamon
1 tsp fresh lemon juice
Salt and pepper

🕐 Prep time: 40 minutes
➤ Calories per serving:
About 505

1 | In a roasting pan, heat oil and brown pork tenderloin on all sides over high heat. Season with salt, pepper, and thyme. Cover and cook on low for 10 minutes (check periodically and turn, to avoid burning).

2 | Rinse plums, halve, and remove pits. Peel and chop onion. Set aside two thirds of the plums. Add remaining plums and onion to the pork and sauté briefly (add more oil if necessary). Add beef stock and simmer for 20 minutes.

3 | Remove pork and keep warm. Purée the plum-onion mixture with the cooking liquid. Stir in crème fraîche and return to pan; cook on low to slightly reduce. Season to taste with salt, pepper, cinnamon, and fresh lemon juice. Add remaining plums and let sauce stand briefly.

4 | Slice pork tenderloin. Serve slices with sauce and plums.

Middle-Eastern
Lamb Chops with Couscous

SERVES 2:

➤ ²/₃ cup couscous

1 cup vegetable stock

2 cloves garlic

¹/₄ cup olive oil

2 double lamb chops (about 6 oz each)

2 cups peas (shelled, fresh, or frozen)

¹/₃ cup fresh mint sprigs

1 pinch cumin

Salt and pepper

🕐 Prep time: 30 minutes

➤ Calories per serving: About 630

1 | Pour couscous into a bowl. Bring vegetable stock to a boil, pour over couscous, cover, and let stand for about 10 minutes.

2 | Peel garlic and squeeze through a press. In a small bowl, combine garlic, 1 tbs of olive oil, and some pepper; brush onto both sides of lamb chops.

3 | Bring salted water to a boil and blanch peas for 3

minutes. Rinse under cold water and drain well.

4 | Rinse mint and pluck off leaves. Set aside several leaves for garnish and mince remaining leaves.

5 | Sauté lamb chops for 6 minutes using 2 tbs of olive oil. Toss couscous, peas, and mint with remaining 1 tbs olive oil. Season with salt, pepper, and cumin. Serve chops alongside couscous.

Easy
Veal Cutlets with Carrots and Apples

SERVES 2:

➤ 1 bunch carrots (about 1 lb)

1 apple

1 tbs fresh lemon juice

3 tbs butter

¹/₂ cup apple juice or vegetable stock

8 fresh chive spears

2 veal cutlets (about 6 oz each)

2 tbs oil

Salt and pepper

🕐 Prep time: 40 minutes

➤ Calories per serving: About 520

1 | Peel carrots and cut diagonally into slices ¹/₄ inch thick. Peel apple, cut into eighths, remove core, and cut into wedges ¹/₄ inch thick. Drizzle with the fresh lemon juice.

2 | In a pan, melt butter and briefly sauté carrots and apple wedges. Pour in apple juice and simmer for 10 minutes. Season with salt and pepper. Rinse chives, chop into rings, and stir into contents of pan.

3 | Cut each veal cutlet in half and sauté in hot oil for 5 minutes on each side. Season with salt and pepper. Serve vegetables with the meat.

◄ *Photo top:* **Lamb Chops with Couscous**   *Photo bottom:* **Veal Cutlets with Carrots and Apples**

Low-Fat | Elegant
Cod with Oranges

SERVES 2:

➤ $3/4$ lb cod fillet
Juice of $1/2$ lemon
2 fennel bulbs
(about $1/2$ lb)
3 tbs olive oil
1 tsp fennel seeds
1 cup dry white wine
(or fish stock)
2 oranges
10 pitted black olives
Salt and pepper

🕐 Prep time: 45 minutes
➤ Calories per serving:
About 450

1 | Rinse cod fillet under cold water, pat dry, and cut into 1-inch cubes. Drizzle with lemon juice and season with salt and pepper. Cover and refrigerate.

2 | Rinse fennel. Cut off greens, chop finely, and set aside. Cut fennel bulb into narrow strips. In a pan, heat 2 tbs of olive oil and sauté fennel briefly. Season with salt, pepper, and fennel seeds.

Pour in white wine, cover, and simmer for 10 minutes.

3 | Peel oranges with a sharp paring knife so that all the white membrane is removed. Remove orange segments from inner membrane and cut into small pieces. Chop pitted olives coarsely and distribute with orange pieces on top of fennel.

4 | In a pan, heat remaining olive oil and sauté cod pieces for 3 minutes. Serve fish alongside or with orange-fennel mixture, sprinkled with fennel greens.

Simple | Refined
Almond-Crusted Ocean Perch Fillet

SERVES 2:

➤ 2 ocean perch fillets
(about 7 oz each)
1 tbs fresh lemon juice
2 tbs flour
$2/3$ cup finely ground almonds
1 egg
$1/4$ cup clarified butter
(specialty store; or make your own by heating the butter and skimming and discarding the white solids)
1 lemon
Salt and pepper

🕐 Prep time: 15 minutes
➤ Calories per serving:
About 725

1 | Rinse fish fillets under cold water and pat dry. Drizzle with lemon juice, season with salt and pepper, and let stand briefly.

2 | Place flour and ground almonds in two separate shallow bowls. Whisk egg in a third bowl. First, dredge fish in flour; then, dip in egg and then in ground almonds, pressing on the breading slightly.

3 | In a pan, heat clarified butter and sauté fish fillets for about 3 minutes on each side, until golden-brown. Cut lemon into wedges and serve with fish.

Exotic | Vegetarian

Indian Vegetable Stew

SERVES 2:

- ➤ 1 onion
  1 clove garlic
  1 piece ginger
  (1-inch section)
  $1/3$ lb carrots
  1 red bell pepper
  $1/2$ lb broccoli
  $1/3$ lb zucchini
  $1/4$ cup clarified butter
  (specialty store; or make
  your own by the heating
  the butter and skimming
  and discarding the white
  solids)
  1 large can tomatoes
  (26–28 oz)
  2 tbs curry powder
  2 tbs grated coconut
  Salt and pepper

- ⏱ Prep time: 45 minutes
- ➤ Calories per serving:
  About 390

1 | Peel onion, garlic, and ginger, and chop. Peel carrots and slice thinly into rounds. Rinse bell pepper, remove interior, and cut into strips. Divide broccoli into small florets and rinse. Rinse and dice zucchini.

2 | In a pot, heat clarified butter and briefly sauté onion, garlic, and ginger. Add tomatoes with juice, mashing some with a fork.

3 | Stir all the rest of the vegetables. Season with curry powder, salt, and pepper. Stir in grated coconut. Cover and simmer for 20 minutes.

Vegetarian |
Sophisticated

Linguine in Lemon Cream

SERVES 2:

- ➤ 2 lemons
  (Meyer if available)
  2 cups frozen peas
  $3/4$ cup fresh basil sprigs
  2 shallots
  1 tbs butter
  1 cup vegetable stock
  $2/3$ cup crème fraîche
  $1/2$ lb linguine
  Cayenne pepper
  Salt and pepper

- ⏱ Prep time: 35 minutes
- ➤ Calories per serving:
  About 940

1 | Rinse one lemon under hot water, zest (avoiding any white part), and squeeze a little juice (reserve zest and juice). Peel second lemon with a paring knife so that all the white membrane is removed (discard peel). Cut lemon segments away from inner membrane and set aside.

2 | Blanch peas in boiling salted water for 1 minute and drain.

3 | Rinse basil, cut larger leaves into narrow strips, and leave smaller leaves whole. Peel and chop shallots. In a pot, heat butter and sauté shallots briefly. Add 1 tsp of fresh lemon juice, vegetable stock, and crème fraîche; mix well and simmer for 10 minutes.

4 | Boil pasta in salted water until al dente. Heat peas in sauce mixture for 5 minutes, then season to taste with cayenne, salt, and pepper. Stir in lemon zest to taste. Drain pasta and serve with sauce, basil, and lemon segments.

Weekend Menus

Strolling through the market, shopping leisurely, stopping for a cappuccino, and buying yourself a large bouquet of flowers—these are the pleasures of weekends. The same principles apply later on when you're cooking. This is when you can take your time and enjoy a glass of Prosecco while preparing a casual evening feast. If you feel like inviting a few friends, no problem—all of these recipes are easily multiplied.

Cocktails

Tequila Caliente

SERVES 2:

- ➤ ¹/₃ cup Tequila
  1¹/₂ tbs Crème de Cassis
  Juice of 2 limes
  Bitter Lemon mixer (or tonic water)

Stir together Tequila, Crème de Cassis, and fresh lime juice. Pour into a glass over ice cubes. Top up with Bitter Lemon and garnish with lime peel as desired.

Singapore Sling

SERVES 2:

- ➤ 2¹/₂ tbs lemon juice
  2¹/₂ tbs gin
  ¹/₄ cup kirsch (or other cherry brandy)
  Sparkling mineral water

Pour lemon juice, gin, cherry brandy, and crushed ice into a shaker; shake well, pour through a strainer into glasses, and top with mineral water.

49

Fast | Simple

Spaghettini with Herb Mushrooms

SERVES 2:

- ➤ ½ lb oyster mushrooms (or other mushroom)
- 2 shallots
- 3 tbs olive oil
- ⅓ cup Marsala (may substitute mushroom stock)
- ½ cup fresh basil sprigs
- ½ cup fresh parsley sprigs
- ⅓ lb spaghettini pasta
- 3 oz freshly grated Parmesan
- Salt and pepper

◷ Prep time: 40 minutes

➤ Calories per serving: About 590

1 | Rinse mushrooms and pat dry. Discard tough stems, and cut into strips. Peel shallots and chop finely. In a pan, heat olive oil and sauté mushrooms for 5 minutes.

2 | Add shallots, sauté briefly, pour in Marsala, and simmer for 15 minutes. Season with salt and pepper.

3 | Rinse basil and parley, discard any tough stems, and chop. Bring salted water to a boil, cook spaghettini until al dente, and drain. Toss with mushroom mixture, fresh herbs, and Parmesan.

Festive | Refined

Arugula-Crusted Rabbit Fillet

SERVES 2:

- ➤ 1 saddle of rabbit (deboned, a little under 1 lb)
- 3 tbs olive oil
- 1 clove garlic
- 1 cup fresh arugula leaves
- 5 tbs butter
- 1⅓ cups breadcrumbs
- 1 pinch cayenne pepper
- Salt and pepper

◷ Prep time: 40 minutes

➤ Calories per serving: About 840

1 | Preheat oven to 350ºF. Briefly sauté rabbit fillets in 2 tbs of olive oil. Season with salt and pepper. Brush a gratin dish with remaining oil and place rabbit fillets inside.

2 | Peel garlic. Rinse arugula and remove stems. Purée both ingredients in a food processor.

3 | Combine purée, butter, and breadcrumbs and season with salt, pepper, and cayenne. Spread onto rabbit fillets.

4 | Bake (middle rack) for 10 minutes. Turn off oven but leave rabbit in for another 5 minutes. Rabbit should be cooked through. Serve.

DESSERT TIP

PERSIMMON CREAM WITH ALMONDS

- ➤ Spoon fruit from the peels of 2 Hachiya persimmons and purée with 1 tbs fresh lemon juice. Combine with 8 oz low-fat sour cream, ¼ cup sugar, and ⅓ cup ground almonds. Toast 3 tbs sliced almonds until golden-brown (in 350ºF oven or in a dry pan on medium-low heat) and sprinkle over persimmon cream just prior to serving.

Photo top: **Spaghettini with Herb Mushrooms** *Photo bottom:* **Arugula-Crusted Rabbit Fillet** ➤

Crispy | Fresh
Mâche with Smoked Salmon

SERVES 2:
- ➤ 2 tbs sesame seeds
- 1 shallot
- 2 tbs white wine vinegar
- ¼ cup olive oil
- 1 tsp honey
- Salt and pepper
- 2 cups mâche (lamb's ear lettuce)
- 3½ oz smoked salmon

🕐 Prep time: 10 minutes
- ➤ Calories per serving: About 405

1 | In a dry pan over medium-low heat, toast sesame seeds briefly. Rinse and drain mâche. Peel shallots and chop finely. In a salad bowl, combine white wine vinegar, olive oil, honey, salt, and pepper. Add chopped shallots.

2 | Toss mâche in dressing. Serve with smoked salmon and sprinkle with sesame seeds.

Spicy | Fast
Strips of Beef Filet in Chile Sauce

SERVES 2:
- ➤ ¾ lb beef tenderloin filet
- 1 small onion
- 1 clove garlic
- 1 fresh red Fresno chile (or red serrano or red jalapeño)
- 2 large beefsteak tomatoes (about 1 lb)
- 2 tbs oil
- ½ cup fresh parsley sprigs
- 1 tsp balsamic vinegar
- Salt and pepper

🕐 Prep time: 30 minutes
- ➤ Calories per serving: About 350

1 | Cut meat into strips. Peel onion and garlic and chop both finely. Remove stem from chile pepper and cut into strips (for less heat, omit seeds). Pour boiling water over tomatoes, peel, remove seeds, and chop finely.

2 | Briefly sauté meat in hot oil. Season with salt and pepper. Remove from pan, and set aside. In the same oil, briefly sauté onion, garlic, and chopped chile. Add chopped tomatoes and simmer for 10 minutes.

3 | Chop parsley. Season sauce to taste with balsamic vinegar. Heat meat in sauce for at least 5 minutes and then stir in parsley.

DESSERT TIP

RASPBERRY GRATIN

➤ Preheat oven to 350°F. Combine ⅔ lb raspberries, 3 tbs sugar, and 3 tbs kirsch or juice. Beat 3 egg whites with 6 tbs powdered sugar until stiff. Fold in ⅓ cup ground pistachios. Separately, crumble 2 oz ladyfingers and mix with 7 tbs cream. Pour cream mixture into a gratin dish, top with raspberry mixture, and cover with the egg-white pistachio mixture. Bake for 15 minutes.

Fast | Sophisticated

Shrimp-Cucumber Salad

SERVES 2:

➤ 1 cucumber

1 onion

$1/2$ lb *cooked* peeled shrimp

Juice of $1/2$ lemon

3 tbs soybean oil
(or other vegetable oil)

1 clove garlic

$1/4$ cup fresh dill

Salt and pepper

🕐 Prep time: 20 minutes

➤ Calories per serving:
About 205

1 | Peel cucumber and grate coarsely. Place in a strainer and press out the liquid. Peel onion and chop finely. In a bowl, combine onion, grated cucumber, and cooked shrimp.

2 | For the dressing, combine fresh lemon juice, soybean oil, salt, and pepper. Peel garlic, squeeze through a press, and add. Rinse dill and chop finely. Add dill and dressing to salad and toss.

For Gourmets

Veal Medallions on Asparagus

SERVES 2:

➤ 1 lb asparagus

4 veal medallions
(about 3 oz each)

3 tbs oil

8 fresh chive spears

$2/3$ cup crème fraîche

3 oz freshly grated
Swiss cheese

Salt and pepper

🕐 Prep time: 35 minutes

➤ Calories per serving:
About 770

1 | Rinse asparagus and trim off tough ends. Blanch in boiling salted water for 5 minutes. In a colander, rinse under cold water.

2 | Preheat oven to 375°F. Heat 2 tbs of oil and fry veal medallions for 5 minutes on each side. Season with salt and pepper.

3 | Rinse chives and chop into fine rings. Stir into crème fraîche and season with salt and pepper.

4 | Brush a baking dish with remaining 1 tbs oil. Place asparagus inside and distribute crème fraîche mixture on top. Top with veal medallions and sprinkle with grated cheese. Bake (middle rack) for 10 minutes. Serve with medallions atop asparagus.

DESSERT TIP

PLUM CRUMBLE

➤ Preheat oven to 375°F. Cut 1 lb plums in half, remove pits and, if desired, mix with $1/4$ cup cognac or other brandy. Place in a baking dish. Beat 2 eggs with $1/4$ cup sugar until foamy. Pour over plums. Mix 4 tbs butter, $1/4$ cup sugar and $1/3$ cup ground almonds until mixture forms small crumbs. Sprinkle over plums. Bake for 15–20 minutes and serve while hot.

For Gourmets

Duck Breast Fillets with Chinese Cabbage

SERVES 2:

- ➤ **2 duck breast fillets (about 1 lb)**
  3 tbs oil
  2 shallots
  1 small head Chinese cabbage (about 1 lb)
  1 tbs toasted sesame oil
  Juice of 1 lime
  $\frac{1}{2}$ cup vegetable stock
  1 tbs soy sauce
  1 tbs sesame seeds
  Salt and pepper

- ⏱ Prep time: 40 minutes
- ➤ Calories per serving: About 930

1 | Rub duck breast fillets with salt and pepper. Heat 1 tbs of oil and sauté duck breasts for 10 minutes with the meat side down.

2 | Peel shallots and chop finely. Rinse Chinese cabbage and cut into narrow strips. In a second pan, heat remaining oil along with the sesame oil and briefly sauté shallots and Chinese cabbage.

3 | Add about 1 tbs fresh lime juice and the vegetable stock; simmer for 10 minutes. Stir in soy sauce and sesame seeds.

4 | Sauté duck breast fillets for another 10 minutes with the skin side down (use more oil if necessary). Make sure they're cooked through. Slice and serve alongside Chinese cabbage.

Can Prepare in Advance

Smoked Haddock Timbales

SERVES 2:

- ➤ **$\frac{1}{2}$ lb smoked haddock (or smoked trout)**
  $\frac{1}{2}$ cup fresh basil sprigs
  1 tsp fresh lemon juice
  $\frac{1}{2}$ lb cherry tomatoes
  3 tbs olive oil
  2 tbs balsamic vinegar
  1 tsp honey
  1 clove garlic

Salt and pepper

- ⏱ Prep time: 30 minutes
- ➤ Calories per serving: About 355

1 | Remove skin or bones from smoked fish. Discard tough stems from basil. Set aside half the basil and finely purée remaining basil with the smoked fish. Season with fresh lemon juice, salt, and pepper and combine.

2 | Rinse cherry tomatoes, cut in half, and place in a bowl along with basil leaves. Combine olive oil, balsamic vinegar, salt, pepper, and honey. Peel garlic, squeeze through a press, and add. Pour mixture over tomatoes; combine.

3 | Using a tablespoon, shape puréed haddock into oval shaped balls, and serve alongside cherry tomatoes.

DESSERT TIP

CANDIED MANGOS WITH COCONUT

- ➤ Dissolve $\frac{1}{2}$ cup sugar in $\frac{1}{2}$ cup hot water. Peel 2 ripe mangos, cut fruit away from pit, and dice. Simmer in sugar syrup for 5 minutes. Stir in 2 tbs rum (optional) and the juice of 1 lime. Refrigerate. Beat $\frac{1}{2}$ cup heavy cream (add 1 tbs sugar near the end) and fold in $\frac{1}{4}$ cup grated coconut. Serve with mangos.

Simple | Fast

Zucchini Salad

SERVES 2:

➤ 1/2 lb small zucchini

1/3 lb carrots

3/4 cup fresh pepper cress, mizuna, or chervil

1/2 pink grapefruit

3 tbs oil

1 pinch cayenne pepper

1 cup fresh arugula leaves

3 oz prosciutto, serrano, or other cured meat (shaved)

Salt and pepper

⏱ Prep time: 15 minutes

➤ Calories per serving: About 505

1 | Rinse zucchini. Peel carrots. Grate both vegetables coarsely into a bowl. Rinse pepper cress and tear leaves into the bowl.

2 | Squeeze juice from grapefruit. Combine juice, oil, salt, pepper, and cayenne; pour over zucchini, carrots, and cress; toss.

3 | Rinse arugula, remove stems, and chop coarsely. Cut cured meat into strips. Add arugula and cured meat to vegetable mixture; combine and serve.

For Gourmets

Salmon with Leek Sauce

SERVES 2:

➤ 1 lb leeks

4 tbs butter

1/3 cup dry white wine (may substitute vegetable stock)

2/3 cup crème fraîche

2 salmon steaks (about 1 lb total)

Salt and pepper

⏱ Prep time: 30 minutes

➤ Calories per serving: About 850

1 | Rinse leeks thoroughly and slice thinly crosswise (rinse slices again and drain); sauté briefly in 2 tbs butter. Add wine and simmer until reduced by half. Stir in crème fraîche and simmer on very low for 8 minutes. Season with salt and pepper to taste.

2 | Rinse salmon under cold water and pat dry. In a second pan, cook the salmon on both sides in remaining butter for about 4 minutes on each side or until nearly opaque throughout. Season with salt and pepper and serve with leek sauce.

DESSERT TIP

HAZELNUT CREAM

➤ Toast 3/4 cup chopped hazelnuts until golden-brown (dry pan over medium heat). Pour in 2/3 cup cream and bring to a boil. Stir in 1 tbs honey and 1 pinch cinnamon. Remove from heat, let cool, and refrigerate. Rinse and dry 4 fresh figs and cut into quarters. Simmer in 1/4 cup port (or grape juice) for 5 minutes. Remove and simmer cooking liquid until reduced by half. Serve figs with hazelnut cream mixture and drizzle with the port reduction.

Photo top: **Zucchini Salad**   *Photo bottom:* **Salmon with Leek Sauce** ➤

Using this Index

To help you find recipes containing certain ingredients more quickly, this index lists favorite ingredients (such as salmon and tomatoes) in bold type, followed by the corresponding recipes.

ABBREVIATIONS

lb = pound
oz = ounce
tsp = teaspoon
tbs = tablespoon

The Author

Cornelia Adam earned her degree as a hotelier and then traveled to England and France to study foreign languages. When she returned to Germany, she became an assistant and later an editor in the food department of a noted German women's magazine. In 1986 she began working as a freelance food journalist. Adam has 50 titles to her credit.

The Photographer

After completing his studies at a Berlin photography school, **Michael Brauner** worked as an assistant to renowned photographers in France and Germany before striking out on his own in 1984. His unique style, coming out of his studio in Karlsruhe, is highly valued by advertising firms and noted German publishers, such as GU.

Photo Credits

FoodPhotographie Eising, Martina Görlach: cover photo

Stockfood Eising, Munich: page 7, top left and top center

All others: Michael Brauner, Karlsruhe

Published originally under the title Kochen für Zwei: schnell was Leckeres © 2002 Gräfe und Unzer Verlag GmbH, Munich. English translation for the U.S. market © 2003, Silverback Books, Inc.

Food editor: Kelsey Lane

Managing editor: Birgit Rademacker

Editor: Tanja Dusy

Reader: Lynda Zuber Sassi and Béatrice Ballin

Layout, typography, and design: Independent Medien Design, Munich

Translation: Christie Tam

Typesetting and production: Patty Holden and Helmut Giersberg

Printed in Singapore

ISBN 978-1-930603-77-6

Enjoy Other Quick & Easy Books

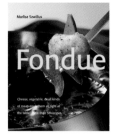

Marlisa Szwillus

Fondue

Cheese, vegetable, or all kinds of meats—enjoy them all right at the table. More than 50 recipes.

Cornelia Adam

Salads

An array of salads to eat as appetizers, entrées, and party dishes. Includes classic choices and cutting-edge alternatives.

Sandwiches

Xenia Burgtorf

Cornelia Adam

Quiche

Delicious, savory pies with vegetables, meat, poultry or fish—serve for all occasions

Cornelia Adam

Garlic

Sophisticated Recipes with this Favorite Spice of the Mediterranean & Beyond. Spicy (tangy), Fine (delicate), International

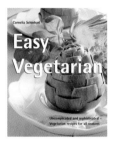

Cornelia Schinharl

Easy Vegetarian

Uncomplicated and sophisticated – Vegetarian recipes for all seasons

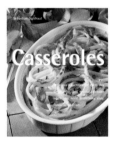

Sebastian Dickhaut

Casseroles

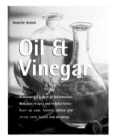

Annette Heisch

Oil & Vinegar

A wonderful source of information, delicious recipes and helpful hints— liven up your favorite dishes and create tasty sauces and dressings.

Andreas Fürtmayr

Sushi

Classic ideas from Japan and new fusion sushi. Home-made perfectly.

1 Noodle, 50 Sauces

Everyday Pasta • Old and New Italian Dishes Noodle biography • 10 Tips for Success

Healthy Wok

Elisabeth Döpp
Christian Willrich
Joern Rebbe

Great for light and satisfying meals

Antje Gruener

Grilling

Crisp, flavorful and hot—irresistible morsels from the grill that do have fixed, from spareribs to skewered vegetables, with sauces and chutneys.

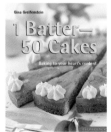

Gina Greifenstein

1 Batter— 50 Cakes

Baking to your heart's content

Cooking in Clay

Healthy Recipes with Great Flavor

Erika Casparek-Türkkan

Doris Muliar

Cocktails for Drivers

100% Enjoyment

Antipasti and Tapas

Mediterranean Appetizers
Cornelia Schinharl

Soups

Classic to Contemporary

Sebastian Dickhaut

Claudia Schmidt

Raclette

New Recipes with Cheese Primer and Party Dips

FLOWERS

➤ Edible flowers are an outstanding, colorful garnish; for example, nasturtium blossoms, which range from light yellow to deep orange, and small blue borage blossoms, which are fantastic on salads, cold dishes, and soups.

Successful Cooking for Two

APPETIZERS FOR MUNCHING

➤ Arrange munchy vegetables such as carrots, kohlrabi, celery, cucumbers (all cut into sticks) and broccoli or cauliflower florets, grouped on a platter, and serve with extra virgin olive oil and coarse sea salt for dipping.

GARNISHING WITH CROUTONS

➤ Depending on your mood and the occasion, cut toasted bread slices with small heart- or star-shaped cookie cutters—cook in some hot olive oil until crispy; serve with soups or salads.

WINE PAIRING

➤ In the spring and summer and for lunches, light dishes paired with white wines work best. Examples: Riesling, Sauvignon Blanc, Chardonnay. Red wines are best during the cozy fall and winter months, such as Cabernet Sauvignon, Pinot Noir, Zinfandel, Bordeaux, and many others. That said, rules are made to be broken and you should experiment with your favorite combinations.